100 Easy Classical Guitar pieces

Book 1&2

Compiled and edited by
Dmitrijs Volkovs

Access to Online Audio
Book 1: https://esmistudio.com/guitarbook1.zip
Book 2: https://esmistudio.com/guitarbook2.zip

ISBN: 978-1-7637136-2-8

Copyright © 2024 Dmitrijs Volkovs

ISBN: **978-1-7637136-2-8**

CONTENTS

1 Renaissance Era Composers

 4 What if a day, or a month, or a year *(Anonymous)*
 5 Branle anglaise *(Emmanuel Adriansen)*
 6 Canary dance *(Anonymous)*
 7 Greensleeves *(Anonymous)*
 8 Pavane *(Anonymous)*
10 Allemande *(Anonymous)*
11 Pezzo Tedesco *(Anonymous)*
12 Toy *(Francis Cutting)*
13 Packington's Pound *(Francis Cutting)*
15 Mr. Dowland's Midnight *(John Dowland)*
16 Orlando Sleepeth *(John Dowland)*
17 Allemande *(Anonymous)*
18 Balletto *(Anonymous)*
19 Galliarde *(Anonymous)*
20 Pavane *(Anonymous)*
21 Air *(Thomas Robinson)*
22 Galliard *(Emmanuel Adriaenssen)*
26 Wilson's_Wilde *(Anonymous)*
28 Alman *(Robert Johnson)*
30 Pavane I *(Luys Milan)*
32 My Lord Willoughby's Welcome Home *(John Dowland)*

37 Baroque Era Composers

41 Aria *(Henry Purcell)*
42 Paradetas *(Gaspar Sanz)*
43 Rujero *(Gaspar Sanz)*
44 Bourree *(Johann Krieger)*
45 Gigue *(Johann Anton Logy)*
46 Bourree *(Leopold Mozart)*
47 Menuet *(Johann Christoph Friederich Bach)*
48 Menuet *(Johann Krieger)*
50 Menuet *(Robert de Visée)*
51 Menuet *(Silvius Leopold Weiss)*
52 Españoleta *(Gaspar Sanz)*
55 Menuet in G *(Johann Sebastian Bach)*
57 Gigue *(Giuseppe Antonio Brescianello)*
61 Bourrée - *Suite in D minor (Robert de Visée)*
62 Entree *(Giuseppe Antonio Brescianello)*
64 Preludium *(Robert de Visee)*
66 Allemande *(Robert de Visee)*
68 Sarabande *(Robert de Visee)*
70 Gigue *(Robert de Visee)*
72 Bourree *(Silvius Leopold Weiss)*
75 Sarabande *(Silvius Leopold Weiss)*
77 Menuet *(Silvius Leopold Weiss)*
78 Menuet II *(Silvius Leopold Weiss)*
79 Bouree *(Johann Sebastian Bach)*
81 Gavotte *(Johann Sebastian Bach)*

85 Sarabande *(Johann Sebastian Bach)*
86 Preludium *(Johann Sebastian Bach)*

90 Classical Era Composers

93 Andante 1 *(Ferdinando Carulli)*
95 Andante in C *(Fernando Sor)*
96 Andante *(Fernando Sor)*
97 Andantino *(Ferdinando Carulli)*
99 Andantino 2 *(Ferdinando Carulli)*
100 Ecossaise *(Mauro Giuliani)*
101 Allegro *(Mauro Giuliani)*
102 Etude A minor *(Dionisio AGUADO)*
103 Menuet in A minor *(Dionisio Aguado)*
104 Walz *(Dionisio Aguado)*
105 Waltz *(Ferdinando Carulli)*
107 Moderato *(Anton Diabelli)*
108 Andante 2 *(Ferdinando Carulli)*
111 Etude No.9 op.35 *(Fernando Sor)*
114 Andantino *(Mauro Giuliani)*
116 Andantino 2 *(Mauro Giuliani)*
118 Andante *(Fernando Sor)*
120 Etude n 17 *(Fernando Sor)*
122 Etude n 22 *(Fernando Sor)*
124 Allegretto *(Dionisio Aguado)*
126 Waltz *(Dionisio Aguado)*
128 Waltz *(Fernando Sor)*
129 Menuet *(Fernando Sor)*

131 Romantic Era Composers

135 Allegretto *(Matteo Carcassi)*
137 Allegretto 2 *(Matteo Carcassi)*
139 Andantino *(Matteo Carcassi)*
141 Study in A minor *(Napoleon Coste)*
142 Etude *(Francisco Tarrega)*
144 Etude in G *(Johann Kaspar Mertz)*
145 Ländler *(Johann Kaspar Mertz)*
147 Lagrima *(Francisco Tarrega)*
149 Pastoral *(Matteo Carcassi)*
151 Romance *(Johann Kaspar Mertz)*
153 Study in A minor *(Matteo Carcassi)*
157 Barcarolle *(Napoleon Coste)*
158 Etude *(Napoleon Coste)*
160 Waltz *(Napoleon Coste)*
163 Etude N 1 *(Francisco Tarrega)*
165 Adelita *(Francisco Tarrega)*
166 Etude N 3 *(Mateo Carcassi)*
168 Etude N 16 *(Mateo Carcassi)*
170 Nocturne *(Johann Kaspar Mertz)*
172 Ejercicio *(Jose Ferrer)*
174 Tango N 3 *(Jose Ferrer)*

176 Latin America/Traditional

177 Greensleeves *(Traditional)*
179 Choro *(Domingos Semenzato)*
181 Cuban Dance *(Anonymous)*
183 Romance *(Anonymous)*
185 Choro *(Joao Pernambuco)*
187 Choro N 2 *(Joao Pernambuco)*
189 Lagrima *(Joao Pernambuco)*
192 Yolanda *(Domingos Semenzato)*

Renaissance Composers

Anonymous

The Renaissance (which means "rebirth or "revival") began around 1400 and ended in the early 1600s. The musicians and artists of the Renaissance looked back to classical models, spawning a new era of artistic growth. With the invention of the printing press, music became available to the public as never before.

John Dowland (1563-1626)

John Dowland was an English Renaissance composer, lutenist, and singer. He is best known today for his melancholy songs such as "Come, heavy sleep", "Come again", "Flow my tears", "I saw my Lady weepe" and "In darkness let me dwell", but his instrumental music has undergone a major revival, and with the 20th century's early music revival, has been a continuing source of repertoire for lutenists and classical guitarists.

Francis Cutting (c.1550–1595/6)

Francis Cutting was an English Lutenist and Composer during the Renaissance period. Renaissance music is European music written during the Renaissance. Defining the beginning of the musical era is difficult, given the gradually adopted "Renaissance" characteristics: musicologists have placed its beginnings from as early as 1300 to as late as the 1470s.

Thomas Robinson (1588-1610?)

Thomas Robinson's was an English renaissance composer and music teacher, who flourished around 1600. He taught and wrote music for lute, cittern, orpharion, bandora, viol, and singing. His works for the most part consist of his own compositions.

Emmanuel Adriaenssen (1554-1604)

Emmanuel Adriaenssen was a Flemish lutenist and influential author of Pratum Musicum. This contains lute solos, and more importantly settings of madrigals for multiple lutes and different ensembles involving lutes and voices giving much study material for the researcher into renaissance performance practice. The ensemble pieces have been recorded by the Dowland Consort of Lutes.

Robert Johnson (1583-1634)

Robert Johnson was an English composer and lutenist of the late Tudor and early Jacobean eras. He is sometimes called "Robert Johnson II" to distinguish him from an earlier Scottish composer. He worked with William Shakespeare providing music for some of his later plays.

Luis de Milán (c. 1500 – c. 1561)

Luis de Milán (c. 1500 – c. 1561) was a Spanish Renaissance composer, vihuelist, and writer on music. He was the first composer in history to publish music for the vihuela de mano, an instrument employed primarily in the Iberian peninsula and some of the Italian states during the 15th and 16th centuries, and he was also one of the first musicians to specify verbal tempo indications in his music.

What if a day, or a month, or a year.

Traditional (XVI century)

Branle anglais

Emmanuel Adriansen (1550-1604)

Canary dance

Anonymous (XVIII century)

Greensleeves

16th century English Traditional

Pavane

Anonymous (XVI century)

2

Allemande

Anonymous XVI century

Pezzo Tedesco

Anonymous 16th century

Toy

Francis Cutting (ca.1550-1595/1596)

Packington's Pound

Francis Cutting
(ca.1550-1595/1596)

Mr. Dowland's Midnight

John Dowland (1563-1626)

Orlando Sleepeth

John Dowland (1561-1626)

Allemande

Anonymous XVI century

Balletto

Anonymous XVI century

Galliarde

Anonymous XVI century

Pavane

Anonymous XVI century

AIR

Thomas Robinson (1560-1610)

Galliard

Emmanuel Adriaenssen (1550-1604)

Wilson's Wilde

Anonymous XVI century

Alman

Robert Johnson (1583-1633)

29

Pavane I

Luys Milán (1500 - 1562)

My Lord Willoughby's Welcome Home

John Dowland (1563-1626)

Baroque Composers

Henry Purcell (1659-1695)

Henry Purcell was an English organist and Baroque composer of secular and sacred music. Although Purcell incorporated Italian and French stylistic elements into his compositions, his legacy was a uniquely English form of Baroque music.

Gaspar Sanz (1640-1710)

Gaspar Sanz was an Aragonese composer, guitarist, organist and priest born to a wealthy family in Calanda in the Spanish comarca of Bajo Aragón. He studied music, theology and philosophy at the University of Salamanca, where he was later appointed Professor of Music.

Johann Krieger (1651-1735)

Krieger's keyboard music places him among the most important German composers of his time. The two published collections, Sechs musicalische Partien (1697) and Anmuthige Clavier-Übung (1698), contain harpsichord suites, organ toccatas, fugues, ricercars, and other works. Krieger's contemporaries praised his contrapuntal skill, evident in the extant fugues and ricercars. Johann Mattheson was particularly impressed with Krieger's double fugues, remarking that he knew nobody who surpassed Krieger in this form, except Handel. Handel himself admired and studied Krieger's work, even taking a copy of Anmuthige Clavier-Übung with him to England.

Johann Anton Logy (1645 – 1721)

Johann Anton Logy composed mostly dance suites. Losy mastered French **lute** style and his extant works demonstrate his intelligence, bright spirited love for the lute. His extensive and highly creative works are scattered through various archives

Johann Georg Leopold Mozart (1719 –1787)

Johann Georg Leopold Mozart was a German composer, conductor, teacher, and violinist. Mozart is best known today as the father and teacher of Wolfgang Amadeus Mozart, and for his violin textbook Versuch.

Robert de Visee (1655 – 1732)

Robert de Visée was a lutenist, guitarist, theorbist and viol player at the court of Louis XIV, as well as a singer, and composer for lute, theorbo and guitar. Robert de Visée's origin is unknown, although a Portuguese origin of his surname had been suggested. Visée published two books of guitar music which contained twelve suites between them, as well as a few isolated pieces.

Silvius Leopold Weiss (1687-1750)

Silvius Leopold Weiss was a German composer and lutenist. Weiss was one of the most important and most prolific composers of lute music in history and one of the best-known and most technically accomplished lutenists of his day. He wrote around 600 pieces for lute, most of them grouped into 'sonatas' or suites, which consist mostly of baroque dance pieces.

Johann Sebastian Bach (1685-1750)

Johann Sebastian Bach was a German composer, organist, harpsichordist, violist, and violinist whose sacred and secular works for choir, orchestra, and solo instruments drew together the strands of the Baroque period and brought it to its ultimate maturity.

Giuseppe Antonio Brescianello (1690-1758)

Giuseppe Antonio Brescianello was an Italian Baroque composer and violinist. He invigorated musical life in Stuttgart. His contemporaries praised his chamber works. The music of Brescianello shows great sense of melody, profound harmonic imagination combined with strong rhythmic element so typical to Italian school of the time.

Aria

Henry Purcell (1659 - 1695)

Paradetas

Gaspar Sanz (1640-1710)

Rujero

Gaspar Sanz (1640-1710)

Bourrée

Johann Krieger (1651–1735)

Gigue

Johann Anton Logy (1650 - 1721)

Bourree

Leopold Mozart (1719-1787)

Menuet

Johann Christoph Friederich Bach (1732-1795)

Menuet

Johann Krieger (1651–1735)

Menuet

Robert de Visée (1650-1725)

Menuet

Silvius Leopold Weiss (1687-1750)

Españoleta

Gaspar Sanz (1640-1710)

Grazioso ♩ = 120

D.C. al Fine

Menuet in G

Johann Sebastian Bach (1685-1750) BWV Anh. 114

56

Gigue

Giuseppe Antonio Brescianello (1690-1758)

59

Bourrée - Suite in D minor

Robert de Visée (1650-1725)

Entrée

Giuseppe Antonio Brescianello (1690-1758)

Preludium

Robert de Visée (1650-1725)

Allemande

Robert de Visée (1650-1725)

Sarabande

Robert de Visée (1650-1725)

Gigue

Robert de Visée (1650-1725)

Bourree

Silvius Leopold Weiss (1687-1750)

Sarabande

Silvius Leopold Weiss (1687-1750)

Menuet

Silvius Leopold Weiss (1687-1750)

Menuet II

Silvius Leopold Weiss (1687-1750)

Bouree

Johann Sebastian Bach (1685-1750)

Gavotte (from suite 6 for cello, BWV 1012)

Johann Sebastian Bach (1685-1750)

Gavotte II

D.C. Gavotte I

D.C. Gavotte I

D.C. Gavotte I

Sarabande

Johann Sebastian Bach (1685-1750)

Preludium

Johann Sebastian Bach (1685-1750)

88

89

Classical Era Composers

Ferdinando Carulli (1770-1841)

Ferdinando Carulli was born in Naples, Italy on February 10, 1770. Carulli's first musical instruction was on the cello, but he soon turned his attention to the guitar. Carulli was entirely self taught, as there were no guitar teachers in Naples at the time. Despite having no formal instruction on the guitar, Carulli rapidly became known as one of the leading virtuosos of his day.

Fernando Sor (1778-1839)

Fernando Sor was a Spanish classical guitarist and composer. He is best known for his guitar compositions, but he also composed music for opera and ballet, earning acclaim for his ballet titled Cendrillon. Sor's works for guitar range from pieces for advanced players, such as Variations on a Theme of Mozart, to beginner pieces.

Mauro Giuliani (1781-1829)

Mauro Giuliani was an italian guitarist and composer, and is considered by many to be one of the leading guitarist virtuosos of the early nineteenth century. He was a prolific composer, writing over 150 pieces for the guitar, as well as many chamber compositions for the violin, voice, flute, piano, and chamber orchestra.

Dionisio Aguado (1784-1849)

Dionisio Aguado was a Spanish classical guitarist and composer. Born in Madrid, he studied with Miguel Garcia. In 1825, Aguado visited Paris, where he met and became friends with lived with Fernando Sor. Aguado's major work Escuela de Guitarra was a guitar tutorial published in 1825. Dionisio Aguado has attained lasting fame through his method for guitar, which is still in print today.

Anton Diabelli (1781-1858)

Anton (or Antonio) Diabelli was an Austrian music publisher, editor and composer of Italian descent. Best known in his time as a publisher, he is most familiar today as the composer of the waltz on which Ludwig van Beethoven wrote his set of thirty-three Diabelli Variations.

Andante (1)

Ferdinando Carulli

Andante (1) in C

Fernando Sor (1778-1839)

Andante (2)

Fernando Sor (1778-1839)

Andantino (1)

Ferdinando Carulli 1770-1841)

Andantino (2)

Ferdinando Carulli (1770-1841)

Ecossaise

Mauro Giuliani

Allegretto ♩ = 88

Allegro

Mauro Giuliani (1781-1829)

Etude A minor

Dionisio AGUADO (1784-1849)

Menuet in A minor

Dionisio Aguado (1784 - 1849)

Walz

Dionisio Aguado (1784 - 1849)

Waltz

Ferdinando Carulli

Moderato
op. 39, no. 15

Anton Diabelli (1781-1858)

Andante (2)

Ferdinando Carulli (1770-1841)

D.C. al Fine

Etude No.9 op.35

Fernando Sor (1778-1839)

Andante.

Andantino
Opus 50 No.27

Mauro Giuliani (1781-1829)

Andantino
Opus 50 No.28

Mauro Giuliani (1781-1829)

Andante

Fernando Sor (1778 - 1839)

Etude n°17 op.35

Fernando Sor (1778 - 1839)

Moderato.

Etude No.22 Op.35

Fernando Sor (1778 - 1839)

Allegretto

Dionisio Aguado (1784-1849)

Waltz

Dionisio Aguado (1784-1849)

Waltz

Fernando Sor (1778-1839)

Menuet

Fernando Sor (1778 - 1839)

Romantic Era Composers

Matteo Carcassi (1792-1853)

Matteo Carcassi was a famous Italian guitarist and composer. Carcassi began with the piano, but learned guitar when still a child. He quickly gained a reputation as a virtuoso concert guitarist. Carcassi wrote a method for guitar (op. 59) that remains valuable, relevant and interesting, blending technical skills and brilliant romantic music.

Johann Kaspar Mertz (1806-1856)

János Gáspár Mertz was born in Pozsony, Kingdom of Hungary, now Bratislava (Slovakia). A virtuoso, he established a solid reputation as a performer. Mertz's guitar music, followed the pianistic models of Chopin, Mendelssohn, Schubert and Schumann, rather than the classical models of Mozart and Haydn (as did Sor and Aguado), or the bel canto style of Rossini (as did Giuliani).

Napoleon Coste (1805 – 1883)

Napoleon is french and is a major figure in guitar composition of the mid-nineteenth century. Napoleon was taught by his mother at a very early age. Napoleon later became Fernando Sor's student and quickly established himself as the leading French virtuoso guitarist. Napoleon is the first composer to transcribe guitar music of the 17th century to the modern era.

Francisco Tarrega (1852-1909)

Tárrega is considered to have laid the foundations for 20th century classical guitar and for increasing interest in the guitar as a recital instrument. Tárrega preferred small intimate performances over the concert stage. Some believe this was because he played without the nails needed for volume. Others say this was related to his childhood trauma.

José Ferrer (1835-1916)

José Ferrer was a Spanish guitarist and composer, born in Spain. Ferrer studied guitar with his father, a guitarist and collector of sheet music, before continuing his studies with José Brocá. In 1882, he left Spain for Paris in order to teach at the Institut Rudy and at the Académie Internationale de Musique.

This page left blank intentionally.

(to avoid awkward page turns)

Allegretto

Matteo Carcassi (1796-1853)

Allegretto

Matteo Carcassi (1796-1853)

ANDANTINO

Mateo Carcassi (1796-1853)

Study in A Minor

Napoleon Coste (1805-1883)

Etude

Francisco Tarrega (1852-1909)

Etude in G

Johann Kaspar Mertz (1806 - 1856)

Ländler

Johann Kaspar Mertz (1806 - 1856)

Lagrima

Francisco Tarrega (1852-1909)

D.C. al Fine

Pastoral

Matteo Carcassi (1796-1853)

Romance

Johann Kaspar Mertz (1806 - 1856)

Study in A minor

Matteo Carcassi (1796 - 1853)

Barcarolle

Napoleon Coste (1805 - 1883)

Etude No.13

Napoleon Coste (1806 - 1883)

Waltz

Napoleon Coste (1805 - 1883)

Etude No.1

Francisco Tarrega (1852-1909)

Adelita
Mazurka

Francisco Tarrega (1852-1909)

Etude No.3 Op.60

Matteo Carcassi (1796-1853)

Etude No.16 Op.60

Matteo Carcassi (1792 -1853)

Nocturne
Opus 4 No.2 Part1

Johann Kaspar Mertz (1806 - 1856)

Ejercicio

Jose Ferrer (1835 - 1916)

Tango n°3 op.50

Jose Ferrer (1835 - 1916)

Latin America Composers

Domingos Semenzato (1908-1993)

Domingos Semenzato, Brazilian composer and guitarist (1908-1993), began his musical activity as a member of chôros groups playing the guitar and the cavaquinho (a small stringed instrument similar to the Canarian timple). Later, he perfected his classical guitar studies in Sao Paulo, becoming a great soloist.

João Pernambuco (1883-1947)

João Teixeira Guimarães (1883-1947), better known as João Pernambuco, is one of the founders of the Brasilian guitar choro style, and his compositions for solo violão are deservedly considered belonging to the core of classic choro, popular with guitarists, loved and admired by audiences in Brazil and elsewhere.

Greensleeves

16th century English Traditional

Choro

Domingos Semenzato (1908-1993)

Cuban Dance

Anonymous

Romance
Spanish Romance

Anonymous

Choro

João Pernambuco (1883-1947)

Choro n°2

João Pernambuco (1883 - 1947)

Lágrima
Tango

João Pernambuco (1883 - 1947)

Yolanda

(Waltz)

Domingos Semenzato (1908-1993)

www.ingramcontent.com/pod-product-compliance
Lightning Source LLC
Chambersburg PA
CBHW040310100526
44585CB00026BA/2879